Junior Field Gu...

Fishes
of
Nunavut

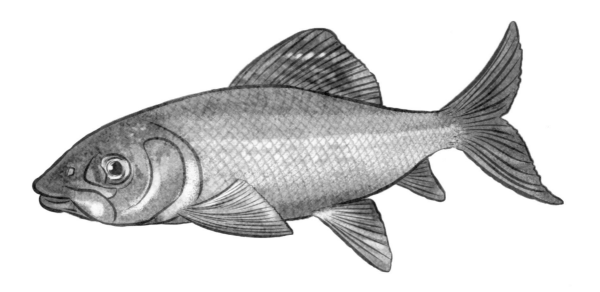

WRITTEN BY
Jordan Hoffman

ILLUSTRATED BY
Ben Shannon

TABLE OF CONTENTS

WHAT IS A FISH?

Fish are a large group of animals. There are more than 30 000 species of fish! There are 1200 species of fish in Canada's waters.

Fish can live in different habitats, including salt water, fresh water, and areas where salt water and fresh water mix.

Fish breathe using **gills**. They get **oxygen** from water as it moves over their gills.

Fish cannot control the temperature of their bodies. Their bodies change temperature depending on how warm or cold the water is.

Fish have scales. Scales are stiff structures that grow out of the skin. Scales provide protection and may help fish swim more easily. Scales can be different shapes and sizes. They also come in different colours so fish can blend in with their environments or stand out from them.

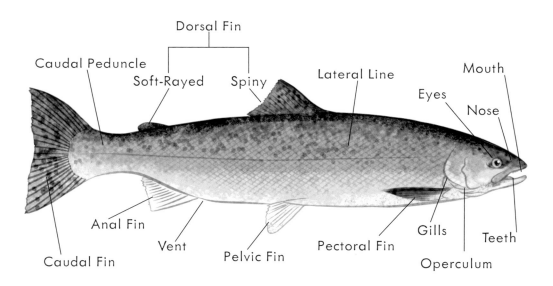

Dorsal Fin

Caudal Peduncle

Soft-Rayed Spiny

Lateral Line

Mouth

Eyes

Nose

Anal Fin

Vent

Pelvic Fin

Pectoral Fin

Gills

Teeth

Caudal Fin

Operculum

Characteristics of fish

- Fish breathe using gills.
- Fish cannot control the temperature of their bodies.
- Fish have scales.
- Fish have fins.

Fish have fins. Fins are used for swimming. Fish need to swim for many reasons. They swim to move to shallower or deeper water, to travel up and down rivers, or to escape predators. Sometimes fins are brightly coloured or have spots and stripes.

There are many different shapes and sizes of fish. Some look like fish you are probably used to seeing, such as Arctic char. Others are long like eels or fat and round like the ocean sunfish.

There are three major types of fish: bony fish, cartilaginous fish, and jawless fish.

Bony fish have skeletons made of bones. Arctic char, lake trout, Greenland halibut, and Arctic cod are examples of bony fish.

Cartilaginous fish have skeletons made out of softer rubbery tissue called **cartilage** instead of bones. Greenland sharks and thorny skate are examples of cartilaginous fish.

Jawless fish do not have jaws. Arctic lampreys and northern hagfish are examples of jawless fish.

Hagfish are jawless fish.

Arctic char are bony fish.

Greenland sharks are cartilaginous fish.

MAP OF NUNAVUT

Most fishes in Nunavut are found all over the territory. This map shows some of the specific places mentioned in the book.

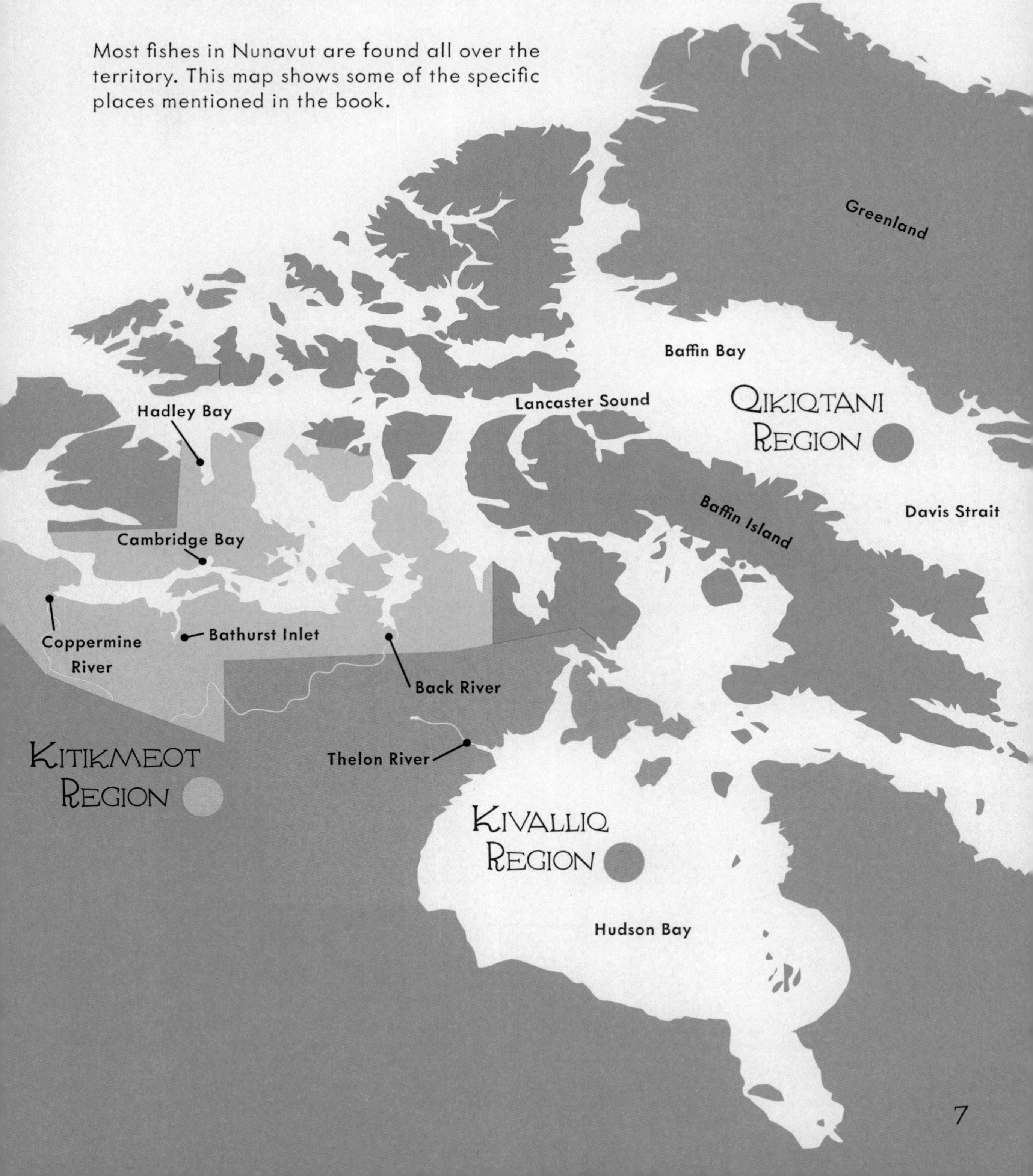

Greenland

Baffin Bay

Lancaster Sound

QIKIQTANI REGION

Hadley Bay

Baffin Island

Davis Strait

Cambridge Bay

Coppermine River

Bathurst Inlet

Back River

KITIKMEOT REGION

Thelon River

KIVALLIQ REGION

Hudson Bay

Arctic char

Appearance

An Arctic char has a long body that is widest near the **dorsal fin**. A dorsal fin is the fin or fins found on the back of a fish.

Arctic char can be different colours depending on where they live, the time of year, and how old they are. An Arctic char usually has a dark green or blue-green back. The sides of its body are generally silver-blue with orange and white spots. It usually has a light-coloured belly, but sometimes it can be orange. Its fins may be orange, red, or gold during **spawning**. Male Arctic char are more colourful than females during spawning. The flesh of Arctic char can be red, pink, or white.

The Arctic char has medium-sized eyes and a rounded snout. It has teeth on its upper and lower jaws and on its tongue. Its scales are tiny and round. The tail fin of the Arctic char is slightly indented at the end of its body. This type of tail fin is called a slightly forked tail fin.

Arctic char usually grow 35 to 60 centimetres long. They usually weigh between 2.3 and 3.2 kilograms, although they can weigh up to 6.8 kilograms in some rivers. Most char that are **landlocked** are smaller. Landlocked fish are found in bodies of fresh water that do not enter the sea.

Range

Arctic char live in waters all over Nunavut.

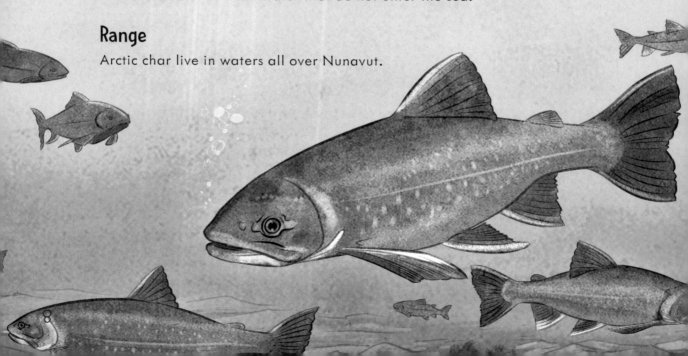

Habitat

Arctic char live in fresh water and salt water. They are usually found in cold, clear water. They stay away from warmer water because it has lower amounts of oxygen.

In fresh water, Arctic char are found in streams, rivers, and lakes. Some Arctic char are landlocked and live in fresh water year-round.

In salt water, Arctic char are usually found near the coast. They like areas where salt water and fresh water mix, such as near the mouths of rivers.

Diet

Arctic char are **omnivores.** They eat **algae, plankton**, shrimp, insects, and small fish. They also eat prey that live on the bottom of water bodies, such as snails and clams.

Some Arctic char are **cannibals**, which means they eat members of their own species. Large Arctic char sometimes eat smaller Arctic char in landlocked freshwater **populations.**

Reproduction and life cycle

Arctic char spawn in fresh water between August and October, usually every other year. Males arrive first to the areas where they spawn. Once they are there, the males create and defend territories. Females arrive later and breed with these males.

When laying its eggs, a female Arctic char chooses a spot where the water is deep enough that it does not freeze all the way to the bottom. There, on a bed of gravel, the eggs are **fertilized** by male sperm in the deep water.

The eggs of Arctic char hatch in early spring. The newly hatched fish get the nutrients they need from their **yolk sacs.**

Behaviour

Arctic char spend their winters in the water beneath the ice in frozen lakes. In the spring, they **migrate** downstream from freshwater areas to the sea. In the fall, they migrate back upstream from the sea to fresh water. Young Arctic char spend the first one to three years of their lives in fresh water before they migrate to the sea.

Arctic char that are landlocked swim more slowly than Arctic char that migrate to the sea.

Traditional knowledge

The Arctic char is traditionally caught using a *kakivaak* (a traditional Inuit fishing spear).

kakivaak

9

LAKE TROUT

Appearance

Lake trout are closely related to Arctic char. They have long, cylinder-shaped bodies.

A lake trout usually has a dark brown, green, or grey back. The sides of its body are lighter than its back. It has pale-yellow or white spots on its sides and fins. Its fins are sometimes orange-red with white along the edges. It also has a white belly. The flesh of lake trout is creamy yellow, orange, or white.

The lake trout has medium-sized eyes and a large mouth. It has teeth on its upper and lower jaws and on its tongue. Its scales are small and round. The tail fin of the lake trout is deeply forked.

Lake trout are usually between 50 and 80 centimetres long, but they can sometimes grow up to 150 centimetres long. They usually weigh between 13.6 and 18.1 kilograms. The record weight for a lake trout is 40 kilograms.

Range

Lake trout live in waters all over Nunavut. They are common in the Thelon River in the Kivalliq region, the Back River in the Kivalliq and Kitikmeot regions, and the Coppermine River in the Kitikmeot region.

Habitat

Lake trout usually live in fresh water. They are sometimes found in salt water in coastal areas or places where fresh water and salt water mix.

Lake trout are usually found in large, deep lakes. They are sometimes found in shallower lakes, large rivers, and streams.

Diet

Lake trout are **carnivores**. They eat fish such as Arctic ciscoes, lake whitefish, Arctic graylings, and sculpins. They also eat insects, shrimp, worms, clams, and snails.

Some lake trout are cannibals. Large lake trout will sometimes eat smaller lake trout.

Other lake trout populations eat only plankton. These lake trout grow slower than lake trout that eat fish.

Reproduction and life cycle

Lake trout spawn in late summer and fall. Spawning takes place in shallow areas of lakes or in large, clear rivers.

Female lake trout lay their eggs in protected areas, where there is gravel, larger stones, and scattered boulders. These areas often have waves and currents that supply oxygen to the eggs and keep them clear of debris.

The eggs hatch between February and April. Young lake trout stay in shallow areas until the water starts to warm. Then they move to deeper, cooler waters.

Adult lake trout may spawn every year or every two to three years.

Behaviour

Adult lake trout are usually found alone, although they sometimes live in small groups with other lake trout that are the same size. They are not very active.

Lake trout do not migrate. At night, young lake trout sometimes travel from the bottom of lakes or rivers to the surface to feed. Adult lake trout feed early in the morning and late in the evening.

Did you know?

Lake trout often live for more than 20 years. Some lake trout have even lived to be 50 years old!

Did you know?

Lake trout sometimes eat small mammals such as lemmings!

LAKE WHITEFISH

Appearance

A lake whitefish has a long body. It has a dark blue, dark brown, or green-brown back. The sides of its body are silver, and its belly is white. Its fins are clear or dark with light spots.

The lake whitefish has a small head with large eyes and a long snout. It does not have teeth. Its tail fin is deeply forked. It has very large, round scales. Older lake whitefish have humps on their backs.

Most lake whitefish grow to 40 to 50 centimetres long, but sometimes they reach up to 80 centimetres. They usually weigh between 0.9 and 1.8 kilograms but can reach up to 19 kilograms.

Range

Lake whitefish live in waters all over Nunavut, but they are not usually found in the High Arctic.

young lake whitefish

Habitat

Lake whitefish can live in fresh water and salt water, but they prefer water that is not too salty. They can be found in shallow areas and water up to 130 metres deep.

Lake whitefish are usually found in cold lakes. They are sometimes found in large rivers.

Lake whitefish that live in the sea are usually found in shallow coastal areas where salt water and fresh water mix.

Diet

Lake whitefish are carnivores. They feed mainly at the bottom of water bodies. They eat prey such as clams, snails, insects, worms, fish, and fish eggs. Some lake whitefish are cannibals.

Did you know?

Although lake whitefish usually do not live past 20 years old, some have been found that are 48 years old!

Reproduction and life cycle

Lake whitefish spawn from late September to October in fresh water. In lakes, the fish spawn over rocky ridges. In rivers, lake whitefish spawn in shallow moving water with different sizes of rocks.

Female lake whitefish release their eggs into the water, where they are fertilized. The fertilized eggs settle on the bottom in cracks and crevices. The eggs stay on the bottom through the winter and hatch in early spring.

Young lake whitefish stay in fresh water for two to three years while they develop. They sometimes migrate to coastal areas that have a mix of salt water and fresh water.

Lake whitefish become adults when they are around 25 centimetres long, which they reach between 7 and 13 years old. Adult lake whitefish spawn every two to three years.

Behaviour

Lake whitefish that live in lakes are usually not very active. They sometimes migrate short distances from deep water to shallower water in the spring. They migrate back to colder, deeper water in the summer as the temperature increases.

Some lake whitefish populations migrate between fresh water and coastal areas of the sea for feeding.

ARCTIC CISCO

Appearance

An Arctic cisco has a long, slim body. It has a light green, dark green, or brown back. The sides of its body and belly are silver. It has darker dorsal and tail fins. The other fins are pale and appear clear.

The Arctic cisco has a small head and small eyes. Its upper and lower jaws are the same length. It does not have any teeth. The tail fin of the Arctic cisco is deeply forked. This fish has large scales.

Adult Arctic ciscoes are usually around 47 centimetres long, but they can grow to be up to 65 centimetres long. They usually weigh about 1 kilogram, but they can weigh up to 2 kilograms.

Range

Arctic ciscoes live mainly in the Kitikmeot region of Nunavut, especially in Hadley Bay on Victoria Island near the community of Cambridge Bay. They are also found in Bathurst Inlet and the Coppermine River near Kugluktuk. They can sometimes be found in the Qikiqtani region, in Lancaster Sound.

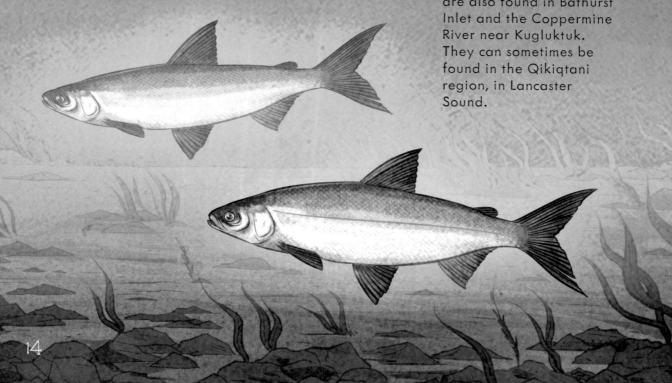

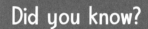

Habitat

Arctic ciscoes can live in fresh water and salt water. They are usually found within 6 metres of the surface.

In fresh water, Arctic ciscoes live in large rivers and at the mouths of rivers.

In salt water, Arctic ciscoes live in bays and in shallow areas near the coast. They can be found in areas where salt water and fresh water mix.

Diet

Arctic ciscoes are carnivores. They eat insects, **crustaceans**, worms, clams, and small fish.

Did you know?

Arctic ciscoes usually live for 10 to 12 years, but sometimes can live up to 24 years.

Reproduction and life cycle

Adult Arctic ciscoes migrate from salt water to freshwater rivers from July to late September. They look for spawning grounds with gravel and clear, flowing water to provide oxygen to fertilized eggs. They spawn in the rivers in late September and October.

Female Arctic ciscoes release their eggs into the water, where they are fertilized. The fertilized eggs stay on the gravel and develop for seven months. The eggs hatch under the ice in the spring.

Young Arctic ciscoes stay near the spawning grounds and feed until the ice melts in May or June. When the ice melts, they are swept downstream into coastal areas of the sea. Young Arctic ciscoes can move offshore within the first year of their lives.

Arctic ciscoes become adults after six to eight years. That is late compared to most fish. An adult Arctic cisco spawns two or three times in its lifetime, usually every other year.

Behaviour

Before they become adults, Arctic ciscoes develop and feed in coastal areas of the sea during the summer.

When they are spawning, Arctic ciscoes can migrate long distances—up to 1500 kilometres!

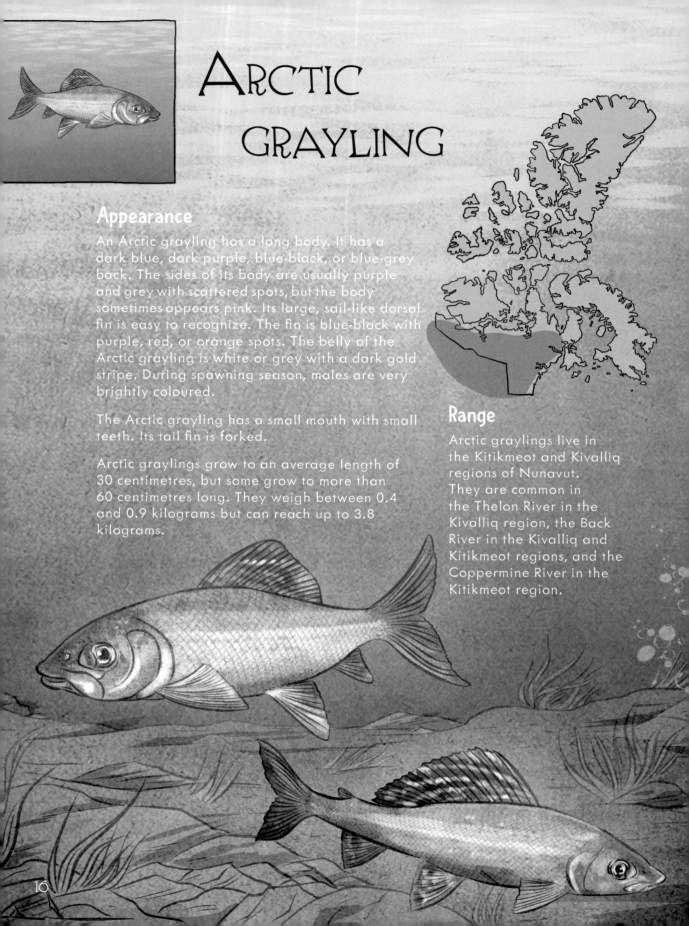

ARCTIC GRAYLING

Appearance

An Arctic grayling has a long body. It has a dark blue, dark purple, blue-black, or blue-grey back. The sides of its body are usually purple and grey with scattered spots, but the body sometimes appears pink. Its large, sail-like dorsal fin is easy to recognize. The fin is blue-black with purple, red, or orange spots. The belly of the Arctic grayling is white or grey with a dark gold stripe. During spawning season, males are very brightly coloured.

The Arctic grayling has a small mouth with small teeth. Its tail fin is forked.

Arctic graylings grow to an average length of 30 centimetres, but some grow to more than 60 centimetres long. They weigh between 0.4 and 0.9 kilograms but can reach up to 3.8 kilograms.

Range

Arctic graylings live in the Kitikmeot and Kivalliq regions of Nunavut. They are common in the Thelon River in the Kivalliq region, the Back River in the Kivalliq and Kitikmeot regions, and the Coppermine River in the Kitikmeot region.

Habitat

Arctic graylings live in fresh water. They like cold, fast-flowing rivers and the bays of larger lakes. Arctic graylings need clear water with high levels of oxygen. They prefer the bottom of water bodies with gravel, larger stones, and places where they can hide. They can also be found in areas with sandy bottoms.

Diet

Arctic graylings are omnivores. Their diet depends on their age and where they live. Young Arctic graylings eat plankton. As they grow older, Arctic graylings eat insects, mollusks, and worms. Adults eat small fish, fish eggs, algae, and plants. They also eat insects, such as bees and beetles.

> ### Did you know?
> Arctic graylings usually live up to 10 years, but some live more than 18 years.

Reproduction and life cycle

Arctic graylings spawn in lakes and rivers in late spring, around the time that the ice breaks up.

In lakes, Arctic graylings spawn in shallow water between 15 and 90 centimetres deep. They spawn in areas with sand and gravel near streams.

In rivers, Artic graylings migrate upstream to spawning grounds in April and May. They spawn in shallow, fast-moving water in areas with gravel and rocks, where the water temperature is between 6 and 12 degrees Celsius.

Arctic graylings do not build nests during spawning, but males defend territories from other males before females arrive at the spawning areas. Once males form territories, females move through the territories to find suitable males. Males try to attract females by covering them with their dorsal fins.

Arctic graylings usually spawn every year. In some northern populations, they spawn every two or three years. They spawn in the same rivers and lakes their entire lives.

Behaviour

Arctic graylings form groups called **schools**. They can usually be found in small to medium-sized schools.

Arctic Staghorn Sculpin

Appearance

An Arctic staghorn sculpin has a long body that is wider near the head and thinner near the tail.

The Arctic staghorn sculpin has a black, brown, or grey back with dark spots. It also has two dark stripes from its back down to its sides. The female has a yellow belly, and the male has a yellow belly with white spots. It also has dark fins with light stripes. Males are more brightly coloured than females.

The Arctic staghorn sculpin has a large head with large eyes. Its mouth is large and wide with small teeth. Its body is smooth except for scales below the large fins on the sides of its body, just behind the gills. Its tail fin is round and not forked.

Arctic staghorn sculpins usually grow to about 26 centimetres long. In Hudson Bay and Greenland, they are larger, growing to about 30 centimetres long.

Range

Arctic staghorn sculpins live in waters all over Nunavut.

Habitat

Arctic staghorn sculpins live in salt water. They can be found at the bottom of the sea, in areas with sand, mud, gravel, and rocky bottoms. They are usually found up to 174 metres deep, but they can be found as deep as 450 metres.

They like water temperatures between −2 and 13 degrees Celsius.

Diet

Arctic staghorn sculpins are carnivores. They eat small **invertebrates**, such as **krill** and worms. They sometimes eat fish.

Reproduction and life cycle

Arctic staghorn sculpins spawn from late fall to winter. Adult females release between 2000 and 5500 eggs during spawning season. The eggs are about 2 millimetres across. The fertilized eggs develop on the sea floor.

After the eggs hatch, young Arctic staghorn sculpins live and feed in the **water column**, the area between the bottom of the water body and the surface. As young sculpins grow, they move back to the sea floor, where they stay as adults.

Did you know?

In the North, sculpins are often referred to as "ugly fish." Can you see why?

Behaviour

Arctic staghorn sculpins burrow into the soft bottom of the sea floor to avoid predators. They are food for seabirds, seals, and other fish, such as Arctic cod.

ARCTIC COD

Appearance

An Arctic cod has a long, slim body. The widest part of its body is just behind its head.

The Arctic cod has a dark brown back and head. The sides of its body and belly are silver. This fish has a speckled pattern on its back and along its sides. It has dark fins.

The Arctic cod has a large head with large eyes. Its lower jaw extends past its upper jaw, with a whisker-like structure on its chin. Its teeth are small and widely spaced. The Arctic cod has scales that are round and very small. It has three dorsal fins on its back.

Arctic cod usually do not grow longer than 30 centimetres, but they can sometimes grow up to 40 centimetres long. There are no differences in the appearance of male and female Arctic cod.

Range

Arctic cod live in waters all over Nunavut.
They can be found farther north than most species of fish.

Habitat

Arctic cod live in salt water. They are usually found near the bottom of the ocean in deep water, at depths of more than 1000 metres. They can also be found at the surface near drifting ice, or sometimes between the bottom and the surface of the ocean.

Arctic cod can also be found near the mouths of rivers, in areas where fresh water and salt water mix.

Diet

Arctic cod are carnivores. They eat small and large crustaceans, such as krill, **copepods**, and worms, and the eggs and young of various species of fish. In winter, Arctic cod living under the ice eat mainly other fish. Large Arctic cod also feed on smaller, young Arctic cod.

Did you know?

Arctic cod only spawn once in their lifetime.

Reproduction and life cycle

Arctic cod spawn in late fall or winter in the High Arctic. They migrate closer to the coast to spawn under the sea ice. Females can release between 9000 and 21 000 eggs at a time, with an average of 12 000 eggs.

Fertilized eggs float to where the water and ice meet. The eggs hatch 30 to 60 days after they are fertilized, usually just before the ice opens up. Sometimes the eggs hatch under the ice, which may help young Arctic cod avoid predators.

Young Arctic cod start feeding after two weeks. They grow and become adults quickly compared to most fish.

Did you know?

Climate change is causing sea ice to melt earlier in the season. This might have a negative effect on Arctic cod because they depend on sea ice.

Behaviour

Arctic cod sometimes live in very large schools in ice-free, shallow bays during the summer. When there is sea ice, Arctic cod are found alone, hiding from predators in cracks in the ice.

Arctic cod sometimes migrate with the movement of sea ice to avoid predators and find food. They may also migrate to deeper waters to avoid predators.

Traditional knowledge

Arctic cod can be caught using hooks and lines in cracks in the sea ice during the spring.

RAINBOW SMELT

Appearance

A rainbow smelt is small and thin, with a long body. It has a pale-green back. The sides and belly of a rainbow smelt are silver, but the sides can sometimes appear pink, blue, or purple. It has clear fins with small dark spots.

The rainbow smelt has a long and pointed snout. It has small teeth on its jaws and larger teeth on its tongue. Its scales are large and round. The rainbow smelt has one large dorsal fin. Its tail fin is deeply forked.

Rainbow smelt grow to an average length of 35 centimetres.

Range

Rainbow smelt live in western Nunavut. They are found from the Kitikmeot region to Hudson Bay.

Habitat

Rainbow smelt live in fresh water and salt water. In fresh water, they can be found in the middle of the water column in deep lakes. In salt water, they can be found up to 400 metres deep.

Diet

Rainbow smelt are carnivores. They eat krill and other crustaceans, insects, worms, and small fish.

Rainbow smelt are also cannibals. Larger rainbow smelt eat smaller rainbow smelt.

Reproduction and life cycle

Rainbow smelt spawn in fresh water. They spawn in rivers or streams after migrating from the sea in the spring. Spawning takes place at night.

An adult female can release between 7000 and 70 000 eggs at once. Two males fertilize the eggs of one female at the same time. Many of the males die after spawning.

The fertilized eggs of rainbow smelt are clear and about 1 millimetre across. They sink to the bottom of rivers or streams. When the eggs reach the bottom, they stick to gravel, rocks, and plants, often in clumps.

Fertilized eggs hatch after 20 to 50 days. Young rainbow smelt are swept downstream into areas where salt water and fresh water mix. They spend the rest of their lives in these areas, or in the sea.

Behaviour

Rainbow smelt can migrate long distances to spawn. Because they travel such long distances, they sometimes start to migrate before the ice melts.

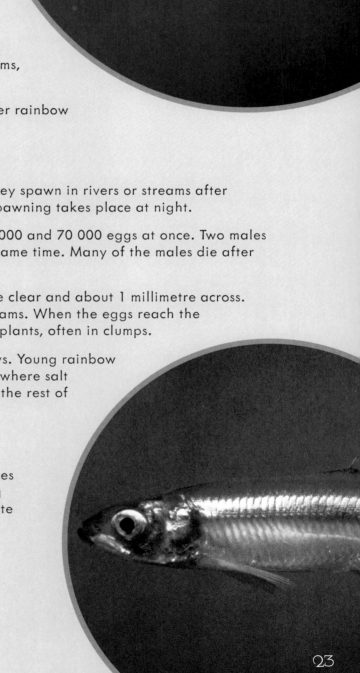

ARCTIC FLOUNDER

Appearance

An Arctic flounder has an oval-shaped body that is flattened. Its back is a green to brown colour and may have black spots. Its belly is white. The fins of an Arctic flounder are pale brown and sometimes have yellow or black spots.

The Arctic flounder has a small mouth and medium-sized eyes. Both eyes are on the right side of its head. The dorsal fin of the Arctic flounder is almost the full length of its body.

Arctic flounder can grow up to 44 centimetres long.

Range

Arctic flounder live in waters all over Nunavut.

Habitat

Arctic flounder live in salt water and sometimes fresh water.

In salt water, Arctic flounder usually live in coastal areas with muddy bottoms. Although they are sometimes found in very shallow water, they usually live near the bottom of deeper bodies of water. They can be found in water up to 90 metres deep.

In fresh water, Arctic flounder sometimes live in rivers. They may also live in coastal areas where fresh water and salt water mix.

Diet

Arctic flounder are carnivores. They eat crustaceans, worms, clams, sea squirts, and other fish.

Did you know?

Arctic flounder can live up to 26 years.

Reproduction and life cycle

Arctic flounder spawn from December to June every other year. Spawning happens close to shore under the ice.

An adult female releases between 31 000 and 230 000 eggs at one time. Arctic flounder do not guard the eggs once they are released.

Male Arctic flounder become adults when they are five years old, and females become adults when they are eight years old.

Behaviour

Arctic flounder move offshore in the fall, then move back closer to shore in the spring. They also move closer to the shore in the evenings when the tide rises.

Arctic flounder are skilled at surprising their prey. They bury themselves in mud and come out at just the right time to catch fish.

GREENLAND HALIBUT

Appearance

A Greenland halibut has a long, diamond-shaped body. It has a yellow or grey-brown back. The belly of the Greenland halibut is pale or dark grey.

The Greenland halibut has a large mouth with teeth on its upper and lower jaws. Both eyes are on the right side of its head and are located far apart. Its scales are small and round. The Greenland halibut has a long dorsal fin that runs most of the length of its body. It also has a tail fin that is only slightly forked.

Greenland halibut grow to an average length of 56 centimetres, but they can reach lengths of 119 centimetres. All Greenland halibut over 90 centimetres long are females. Greenland halibut usually weigh between 11 and 25 kilograms, but they can weigh up to 45 kilograms.

Range

Greenland halibut live in waters all over Nunavut. They are especially common in Baffin Bay and Davis Strait close to the west coast of Greenland.

Habitat

Greenland halibut live in salt water. They usually live in water ranging from 500 to 1000 metres deep, but they can be found anywhere from 1 metre to 2000 metres deep in the sea. They like water temperatures between −0.5 and 6 degrees Celsius.

Greenland halibut prefer areas with soft bottoms made of mud or sandy mud.

Diet

Greenland halibut are carnivores. These predators feed on prey at the bottom of the sea, such as squids, worms, crabs, and shrimp. They are often found in areas that have plenty of shrimp. They also eat fish such as Atlantic cod, polar cod, capelins, and other small fish. Large Greenland halibut also eat small Greenland halibut.

Reproduction and life cycle

Greenland halibut spawn between winter and summer. They can spawn multiple times in a year.

A female Greenland halibut releases between 30 000 and 300 000 eggs at once! The number of eggs released depends on the size of the fish. Larger females release more eggs than smaller females do. Males fertilize the eggs as they are released.

The fertilized eggs of Greenland halibut are clear and 4 to 4.5 millimetres wide. They float in the water column.

When the eggs hatch, young Greenland halibut stay near the surface to about 30 metres deep. As the fish grow, they are carried by water currents and grow into adults at depths of 50 to 200 metres.

Behaviour

Greenland halibut are important prey for marine mammals such as belugas, narwhals, ringed seals, and hooded seals. They are also prey for salmon, rays, and Greenland sharks.

Greenland halibut do not swim with their bodies flat against the sea floor like their relatives do, including Arctic flounder. Instead, they swim with their belly toward the bottom like most other fish. This allows Greenland halibut to swim up to feed on prey in the water column and not just at the bottom of the sea.

GREENLAND SHARK

Appearance

Greenland sharks are the largest fish in the Arctic. They have long, cylinder-shaped bodies.

Greenland sharks have rough skin. Their bodies are black, brown, or grey. Their backs and sides have light or dark spots.

A Greenland shark has a small head, a short, round snout, and small, circle-shaped eyes. It has different types of teeth in many rows. Its tail fin is curved, with a shorter bottom half and a longer top half. It also has two small dorsal fins.

Greenland sharks can grow up to 7.3 metres long. Males are shorter than females. Male Greenland sharks grow to an average length of 3.4 metres, and females grow to an average length of 5 metres. Greenland sharks are heavy. The maximum known weight of a Greenland shark is 775 kilograms!

Range

Greenland sharks live in waters all over Nunavut.

Habitat

Greenland sharks live in salt water. They can be found in shallow waters or at depths of more than 1200 metres. Greenland sharks are known to go as deep as 2200 metres.

In winter, Greenland sharks are usually found near the surface in areas where salt water and fresh water mix, such as at river mouths and in shallow bays. In summer, they live in deeper waters in the sea.

Diet

Greenland sharks are carnivores that eat a variety of prey. They eat marine mammals such as seals, belugas, and narwhals. They eat fish such as Arctic char, Greenland halibut, sculpins, and skate, as well as fish eggs. Greenland sharks are also known to eat squids, crabs, snails, sea urchins, jellyfish, and seabirds. They can also eat the bodies of dead bowhead whales and sharks. They have even been known to eat caribou!

Reproduction

Greenland sharks reproduce very slowly. Adult females give birth to live young, called pups. Females can have up to 10 pups in a litter.

Behaviour

Greenland sharks move very slowly. In the spring, they stay in deep water during the day and swim near the surface to feed during the evening and at night.

Greenland sharks feed very slowly. They take large bites of dead animals' skin, blubber, and meat. Greenland sharks sometimes eat in large groups when there is a lot of food available, such as the meat and blubber of a dead bowhead whale.

Traditional knowledge

Inuit have used the skin of Greenland sharks to make boots and the teeth of the lower jaw to cut hair.

Did you know?

Greenland sharks grow very slowly— only about 1 centimetre a year. They can live to be about 400 years old, though, so they can grow very large!

Did you know?

Small copepods attach themselves to the eyes of some Greenland sharks. The copepods give off light that may lure prey closer to the sharks.

Did you know?

Greenland sharks do not have any known predators in the Arctic.

THORNY SKATE

Appearance

A thorny skate has a flat, diamond-shaped body. It has a long tail that is the same length as its body.

Like the Greenland shark, the thorny skate has rough skin on its back. As its name suggests, the thorny skate also has thorns on its back. Its back is brown-grey in colour, sometimes with dark brown spots. Its belly is white and may have small dark spots. The tail of the thorny skate has a black spot on the tip and is covered in thorns.

The thorny skate has a mouth underneath its body. It has a lot of teeth on its upper and lower jaws. It has a short, triangular snout with two to six thorns on the end.

Thorny skate can grow from 102 to 105 centimetres long. The maximum known weight of a thorny skate is 11.4 kilograms.

Range

Thorny skate live mainly in the waters around Baffin Island, in the Qikiqtani region.

Habitat

Thorny skate live in salt water. They are sometimes also found in areas where salt water and fresh water mix. Thorny skate live at depths ranging from 18 to 1800 metres. They usually prefer to be deeper than 110 metres.

Thorny skate are found mainly offshore and live at the bottom of the sea. They are sometimes found in areas with hard and soft bottoms, but they prefer areas with soft mud, sand, gravel, pebbles, or broken shells.

Diet

Thorny skate are carnivores. They eat worms and small and large crustaceans, such as shrimp and crabs. They also eat fish such as capelins, haddock, and sculpins.

Did you know?

Thorny skate can live up to 28 years.

Reproduction

Thorny skate usually reproduce in the fall. A female thorny skate lays egg cases containing one offspring each. The female usually lays between 6 and 45 egg cases. Egg cases are large, brown-black in colour, and have pointed parts to help them attach to the bottom of the sea or to plants such as seaweed.

Young thorny skate hatch from egg cases when they are between 10 and 12 centimetres long. Adult thorny skate do not protect their young.

Behaviour

Thorny skate are not very active. They usually do not travel more than 90 kilometres from where they hatched. Some populations migrate short distances as the seasons change.

Thorny skate are found in different areas based on their size. Larger fish usually live in deeper and warmer water.

Glossary

algae: a group of plant-like organisms found in water, such as seaweed. Algae can be tiny or very large.

cannibals: animals that eat other animals of the same species for food.

carnivore: an animal that eats other animals for food.

cartilage: a tissue found in the bodies of humans and animals that is rubber-like and softer than bones.

copepods: small crustaceans that live in fresh water and salt water.

crustaceans: a large group of animals that have shells on their bodies. Examples include shrimp, crabs, lobsters, krill, and copepods.

dorsal fin: a fin found on the back of a fish. Some fish have more than one dorsal fin.

fertilizing: the merging of eggs from females and sperm from males. Fertilized eggs will develop into young.

gills: the organs used by fish to get oxygen from the water.

invertebrates: animals that do not have backbones or skeletons inside their bodies, such as spiders, worms, and clams.

krill: a tiny shrimp-like animal that lives in oceans.

landlocked: found in freshwater bodies such as lakes, streams, and rivers that do not enter the sea.

migrate: move from one place to another according to the seasons.

omnivores: animals that eat both plants and animals.

oxygen: a chemical that is in the air and water, has no colour, taste, or smell, and is necessary for life.

plankton: tiny plants and animals that live in large bodies of water, such as the ocean or large lakes.

population: the whole number of people or animals living in a certain place.

schools: groups of fish.

spawning: the time when female fish release their eggs and males release their sperm.

water column: the area between the bottom of a water body and the surface.

yolk sac: a fluid-filled sac that provides nutrients to developing young animals.